How Things Work

How Things Work

What's making it move?

I'm pulling.

Thames & Hudson

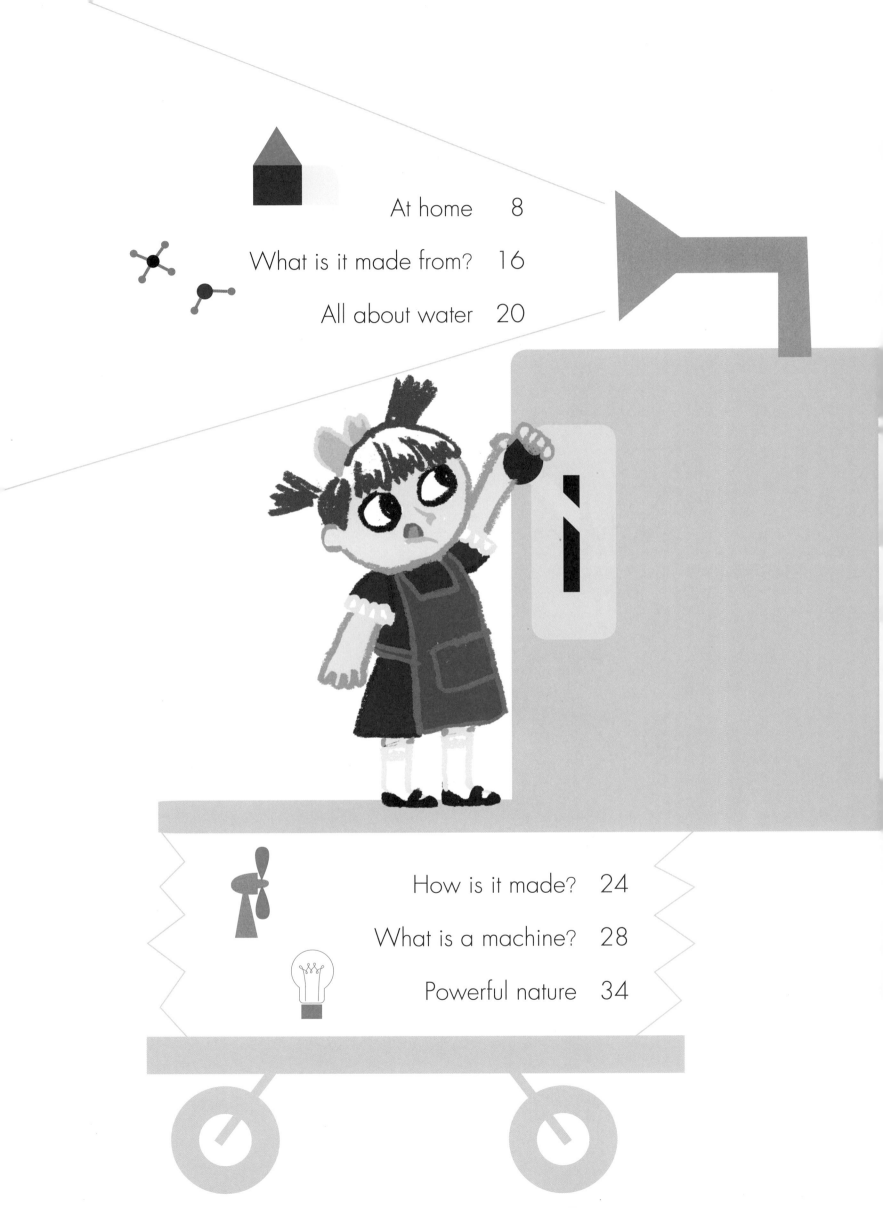

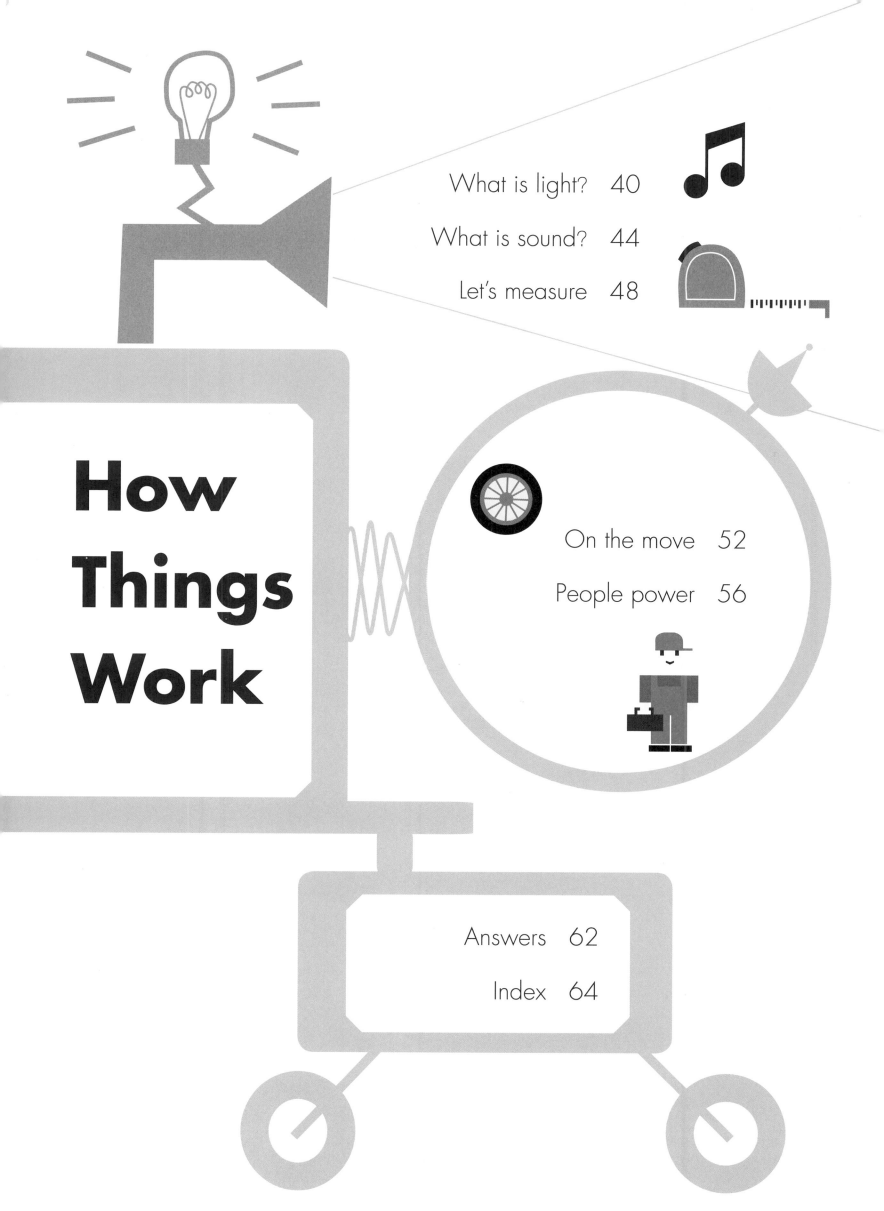

How Things Work

How to use this book

Do you want to find out how things
are made and where they come from?
Get ready to start experimenting.

Say hello to Koko and Alex

I'm Koko. I like
taking things
apart to see
how they work.

I'm Alex.
I want to build
a machine.

Here's our
experiment kit.

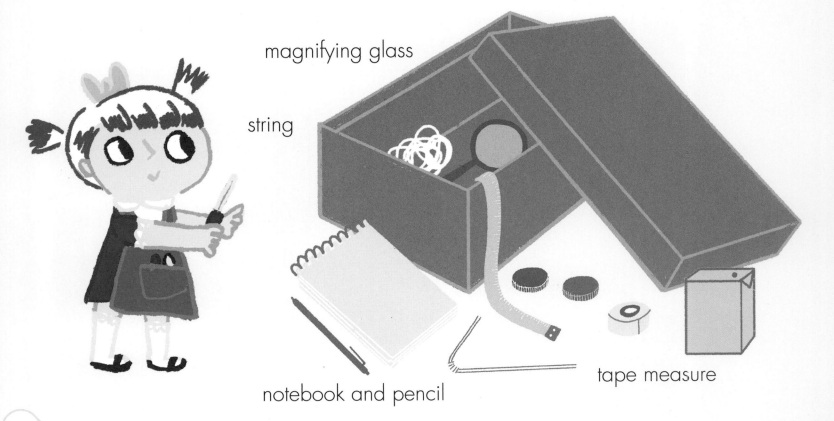

old boxes and cartons

magnifying glass

string

notebook and pencil

tape measure

When you see ...

Adult help needed!

... ask a grown-up to help you.

... get ready to do things.

Meet the explorers

The three explorers love finding things out.
They look, think and ask questions.

I look at things properly.

I ask what will happen next.

I write down what we find out. The answers to the puzzles are on page 62.

OK! Let's go ...

At home
How to build a house

The explorers want to build a new home.

1 This is what we need.

walls

a roof

a door

windows

2 Our house must be strong. Let's build it with bricks, stones, wood and tiles.

bricks

stones

wood

tiles

3 Oh, no! It's raining!

Quick, put on the roof to keep us dry.

We will be warm and dry now!

Let's build a workshop room, too.

Who lives where?

Do you live in a house or an apartment? Are the walls built from bricks or wood? People and animals live in different kinds of homes. Look at the homes in the picture.

I Spy

Play I Spy with your friends. Find different homes in the picture. Here are some to start you off ...

And can you find Foxy?

Power in, waste out!

What happens when you turn on the tap?

What about when you flick on a light switch? Pipes and wires snake into a house to bring clean water and power. They also snake out with the waste.

Use a finger to follow the cables and pipes going into and then out of the house.

IN >> and OUT <<

water pipe >>

waste pipe <<

electricity cable >>

internet/TV/ >>
phone cable

5 ways to save

1

Ask a grown-up to switch off the lights when you leave a room.

2

When brushing your teeth, turn off the tap.

3 TV off …

… when you're not watching it.

4

Wear a sweater inside. Don't turn up the heat.

5

Reuse and recycle.

Energy at home

Your home uses energy 24 hours a day

Lots of things in your home need energy to work. Without energy, you couldn't keep food cold in the fridge or play games on the computer. Look at how Koko and Alex use energy at home over one day.

morning

9:00 am
Koko and Alex go to school!

8:30 am
Alex eats hot porridge for breakfast.

energy meter

8:00 am
Koko brushes her teeth and washes.

How much energy do Koko and Alex use at different times of the day? Look at the energy meter!

red: energy in use

blue: energy not in use

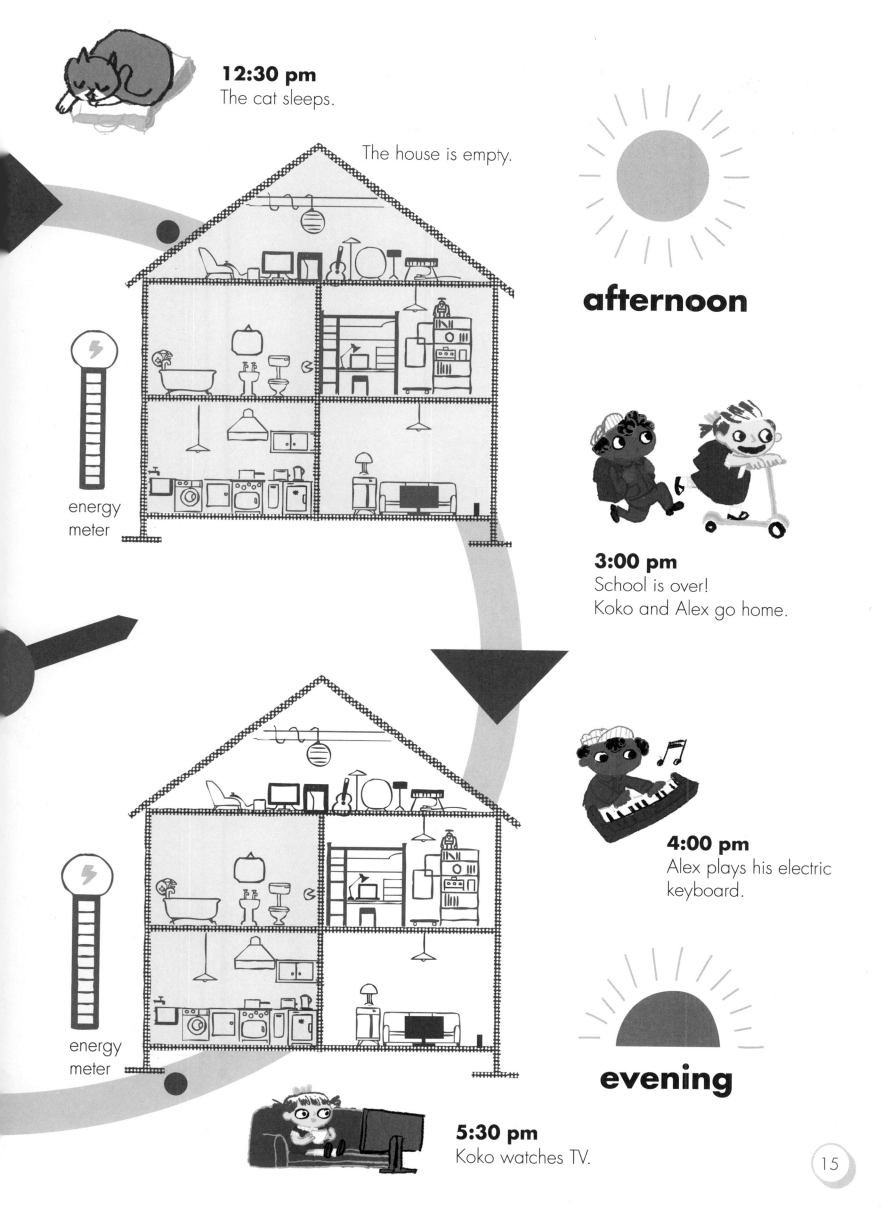

12:30 pm
The cat sleeps.

The house is empty.

afternoon

energy meter

3:00 pm
School is over!
Koko and Alex go home.

4:00 pm
Alex plays his electric keyboard.

energy meter

evening

5:30 pm
Koko watches TV.

What is it made from?

Let's play the material game

What is this book made from? What is a window made from? There are all kinds of materials, such as paper, glass and wood. Lots of toys are made from plastic. A peg is made from two materials: wood and metal. Which materials are the things in the picture made from?

wood
plastic
glass
metal
paper
rock
cloth
rubber
wool

In one minute, point to things that are made of …

… just metal
… more than one material
… paper or rock

Can you ride a bicycle made of wool?

Koko has made some things but she's got the materials all wrong! Can you help her by picking the right materials for the job?

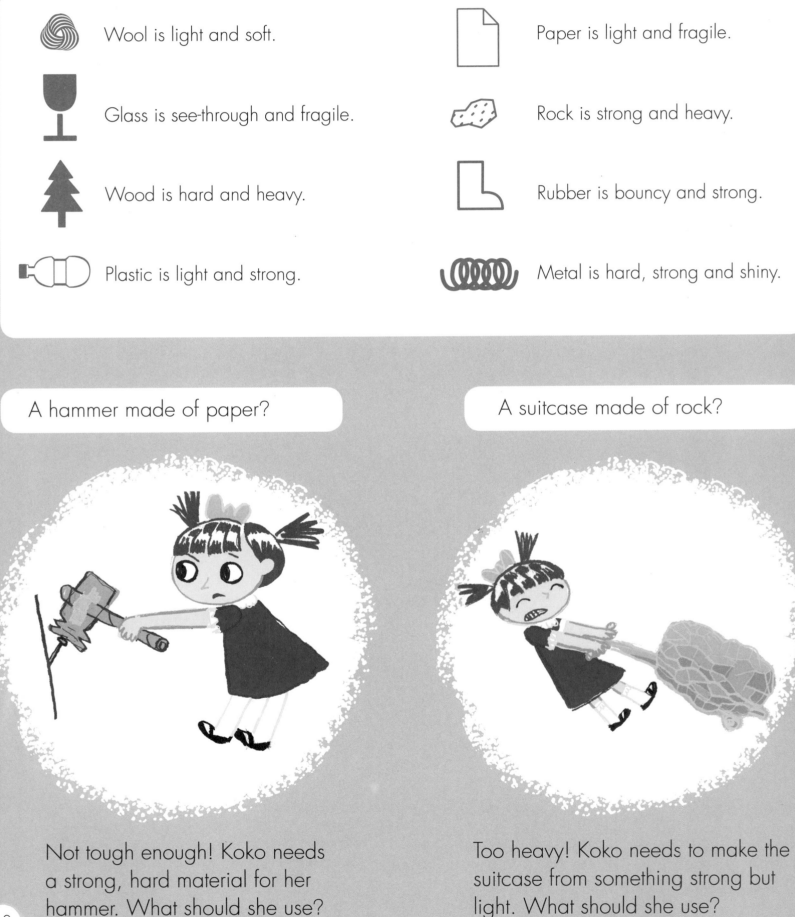

Wool is light and soft.

Paper is light and fragile.

Glass is see-through and fragile.

Rock is strong and heavy.

Wood is hard and heavy.

Rubber is bouncy and strong.

Plastic is light and strong.

Metal is hard, strong and shiny.

A hammer made of paper?

A suitcase made of rock?

Not tough enough! Koko needs a strong, hard material for her hammer. What should she use?

Too heavy! Koko needs to make the suitcase from something strong but light. What should she use?

A bouncy ball made of glass?

Smash! Koko needs a strong, bouncy material to make her ball. What should she use?

A sweater made of metal?

So uncomfortable! Koko needs a soft, light material for her sweater. What should she use?

Glasses made of wood?

No good! Koko needs to see through her glasses so she can look around! What should she use?

A bicycle made of wool?

Too soft! Koko needs to make the bicycle from something hard and strong. What should she use?

All about water
Hot and cold water

Water can change. Let's find out what happens to water when it becomes very cold and very hot.

1 Is water wet or dry? Water from a tap is wet. It is a **liquid**.

2 What happens to the water in an ice-cube tray in the freezer?

3 Water freezes to make **solid ice**.

4 Does the water still look like water from a tap?

5 When ice melts, it becomes liquid again.

6 A kettle heats up water.

7 Boiling water makes **steam**.

8 Look at the steam rising from a boiling kettle. Does the water look like water from a tap?

Never touch steam! It's very hot!

Make funky fruity ice pops!

You will need

an ice-cube tray
pieces of strawberry and banana
apple juice
sticks
a freezer

What to do

1 Place a piece of fruit in each ice-cube space.

2 Fill the tray with apple juice.

3 Leave in the freezer for about 1 hour.

4 Take the tray out of the freezer. Place a stick in each space. Freeze for another 2 hours.

5 Enjoy your funky fruity ice pops with friends!

Adult help needed!

Do oil and water mix?

Let's experiment to find out.

Adult help needed!

You will need

ice cubes

food coloring

cooking oil

jar

What to do

1

Pour some oil into a jar.

2

Put the ice cubes in the oil. Drop food coloring onto each one.

3

The food coloring mixes with the melting ice. Little drops of color sink down through the oil but the oil does not change color. The explorers have proved that oil and water don't mix.

The save water game

When it rains, there's water everywhere! But people, animals and plants need lots of water. We have to save it, not waste it.

Drink water to keep healthy. **Slurp!**

Wash your hands. **Rub scrub!**

START

FINISH

How to play

A game for 2 or more players

1 Place your pieces on **START**. Take turns rolling the die. Follow the instructions on the board.

When you land on
green = save water and move forward
pale blue = enjoy water and pretend to do the action
dark blue = waste water and move back or miss a turn.

2 The first person to reach the **FINISH** is the winner.

Don't take a bath. Take a shower! **Miss a turn.**

Wow! The sun shining through rain makes a rainbow.

Have fun jumping in big puddles. **Splash!**

How is it made?
How was this book made?

Everyone in the OKIDO team worked together to make this book. First of all, the author thought of an idea for each page and wrote the words.

Team OKIDO

Then, at OKIDO headquarters ...

... the photographer took the photographs.

... the illustrator drew the pictures.

... the pictures were scanned into the computer.

... the editor checked the words and the designer made sure the pages looked just right.

The computer files were then sent to the printers ...
Before going there, let's find out about paper.

How is paper made?

Paper is made from trees or recycled from old paper.

Trees are cut into logs and sent to a paper mill.

The logs are blended into a pulp ...

... which is flattened into paper!

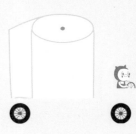

The paper is ready to be delivered to the printers.

What happens at the printers?

At the printers, ink is printed onto paper to make books like this one!

PRINTERS

Look, here on the screen is the page you're reading now!

Let's print! Book pages are printed on a BIG printer.

THE BIG PRINTER

The paper went through the printer on a large roll.

The paper passed under four different colored inks. The colors mixed to make all the different colors you see on the pages.

Finishing touches

The printed pages were cut and folded, then bound together with the cover. The book was finally finished!

The books were delivered to shops ready for you to buy and read.

BOOKSHOP

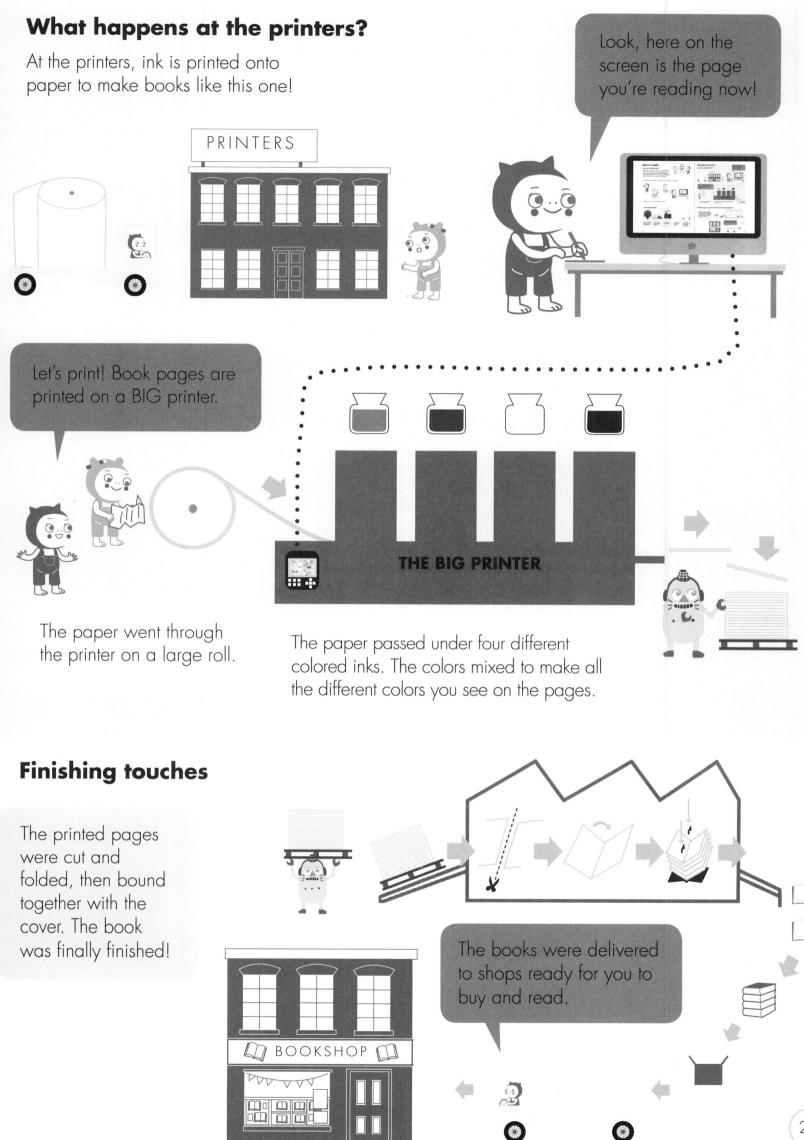

Homemade by you!

Make your own concertina book

Many things you buy in shops, such as books and clothes, are made in factories by big machines. But you can make things at home, too!

You will need

scissors   *paper*

tape

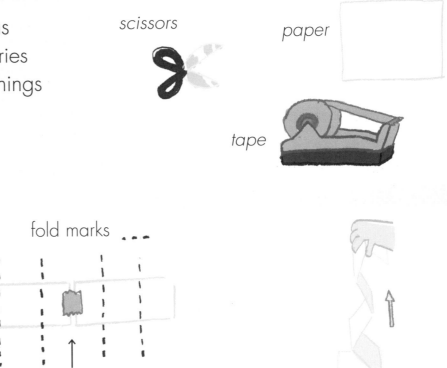

fold marks

cut

tape

1 Cut a piece of paper into two pieces, as shown.

2 Stick the two pieces of paper together. Fold them along the dotted lines shown above.

3 You will have a long concertina-shaped piece cf paper, like this.

Make your own loom

A loom is a machine that makes cloth out of wool or other threads. Make your own loom at home. Turn wool into a beautiful mini-rug!

You will need

4 in x 4 in piece of cardboard
ruler
pencil
tape
different colored wool
plastic needles
round-ended scissors

1 Draw four lines on the cardboard, each one ¾ in from the edge. Draw and cut notches ½ in apart at the top and bottom, making sure the notches match up.

2 Thread a needle with a very long piece of wool. Wind the wool up and down through the top and bottom notches, working your way across the cardboard.

3 Secure both loose ends of the wool with tape.

Adult help needed!

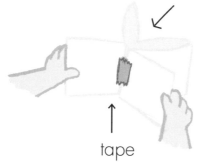

tape

4 Fold the two sides toward the middle, as shown.

5 Stick the two sides together. Push the taped parts of the book together.

6 Close your book as shown. What will you write and draw inside?

Adult help needed!

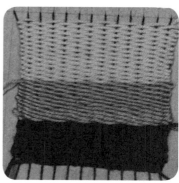

4 Thread a needle with a different colored piece of wool. Work your way from one side of the cardboard to the other, crossing over and then under the threads already in place.

5 Thread another needle with a piece of wool in the same color. Take it over and under the wool threads as before, but go under the threads you went over last time and vice versa.

6 Keep adding rows and alternating the over and under threads so you create your own piece of cloth. Don't pull the wool threads too tight or you'll squish your square!

7 At the end, remove the wool threads from the notches in the cardboard. You can tie the loops at the edges into knots to create tassles for your mini-rug!

What is a machine?

Let's find out with Hedgehog, Rabbit, Little Bird and Squirrel.

1 It had been raining for days and days.

Come and sit in the tree! It's dry up here.

How can we get up there?

It's too high to jump or climb.

2

Let's make a ramp.

THE RAMP

Lean the plank against the tree ...

... and walk straight up!

3 First Rabbit and Hedghog made a gentle slope, but the plank didn't reach high enough.

Let's make a steeper ramp.

Eeeeek!

But it was too steep for Hedgehog to climb.

4

Let's use the plank to make a seesaw catapult! Little Bird, help me test it.

Jump on this end …

… and launch someone into the air!

SEESAW CATAPULT

But when it was Rabbit's turn, no one was heavy enough to catapult him into the tree.

5

Why don't you pull us up with a rope?

Squirrel and Bird pulled on a rope around Rabbit's middle. They pulled until they lifted Rabbit up into the tree! The pulley system machine saved the day.

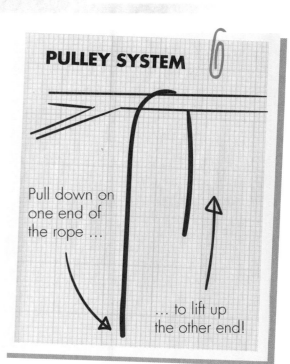

PULLEY SYSTEM

Pull down on one end of the rope …

… to lift up the other end!

6

'My turn!' said Hedgehog. They lifted her easily because she was light.

'Hooray!' they cheered. They sat together in the warm, watching the rain.

Cog mayhem!

How to play

A game for 2 or more players

1 Place your pieces on START.

2 Take turns to throw the die. Check the color of your number on the color key.

3 Move to the matching color space in the first cog.

4 If you land on a solid shape, move to its pair in another cog.

5 If you land on a shape with an outline, don't move.

6 If you roll the same color twice in a row, don't move.

7 The first player to reach the FINISH cog is the winner!

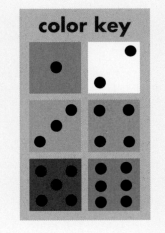

color key

You will need

a die and game pieces

START

30

FINISH

Let's copy nature!

What would you like to invent? A car that flies?
A coat that makes you invisible? Many inventors look
at how nature works and then copy its good ideas.

Built to fly

Airplanes are similar
shapes to bats and birds.

Finding things

Dolphins find fish by sending out sound waves.
People use a similar system called radar to find
out how far away things are and how fast they
are traveling.

Sticky hooks

An inventor noticed that sticky
seeds with tiny hooks stuck to his
dog's fur …

close-up

… so he invented Velcro, which
sticks together but easily pulls
apart. Velcro has many loops
and hooks.

Light and strong

Bees make honeycomb. Look at the shapes.
How many sides are there in each shape?
The shape is strong but honeycomb is light.

Look at the shapes of paper in cardboard.
They are similar to honeycomb.

Make a marshmallow catapult!

Get ready to launch mini-marshmallows at a target!
Ping back a wooden spoon to power marshmallows
or raisins through the air. Aim and fire!

Adult help needed!

You will need

catapult
4 big marshmallows
7 skewers
1 thin rubber band
1 plastic or wooden spoon
tape

ammunition
mini-marshmallows
breakfast cereals or raisins

What to do

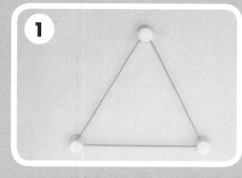

1

Make a triangle with 3 skewers
and 3 marshmallows.

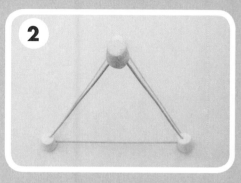

2

Use 3 more skewers and 1 more
marshmallow to make a pyramid.

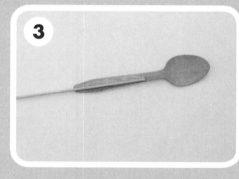

3

Tape a skewer onto the end
of the spoon.

4

Loop the rubber band around the
top marshmallow. Place the spoon-
skewer through the band. Stick it
into the bottom marshmallow.

Ready!

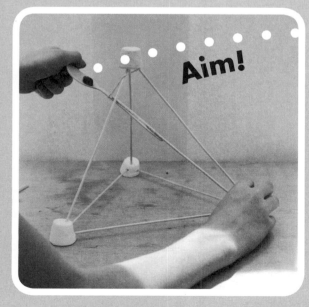

Aim!   Fire!

Gently bend back the spoon,
aim and let go!

Hit!

Powerful nature
Super power! Sun, wind and water.

Special machines take power from nature to make energy. Discover how these machines use sun, wind and water power.

A windmill's sails turn in the wind and make energy to grind grain into flour.

Solar panels soak up heat and light from the sun. They turn energy from the sun into electricity.

Wind turbines spin in the wind. They turn energy from wind into electricity.

A watermill uses the force of flowing water to grind grain into flour.

Let's water the plants! This wind turbine makes energy from wind to pump water into a hose.

Whoa! Waves are fun for surfing but wave machines can also make their energy into electricity.

Make a water wheel

A water wheel is a simple machine that uses the power of moving water. Let's make one and see how it works!

Adult help needed!

You will need

2 bendy straws
a cork
scissors
tape
2 toothpicks
3 pieces of card, each cut to 1 x 1½ in

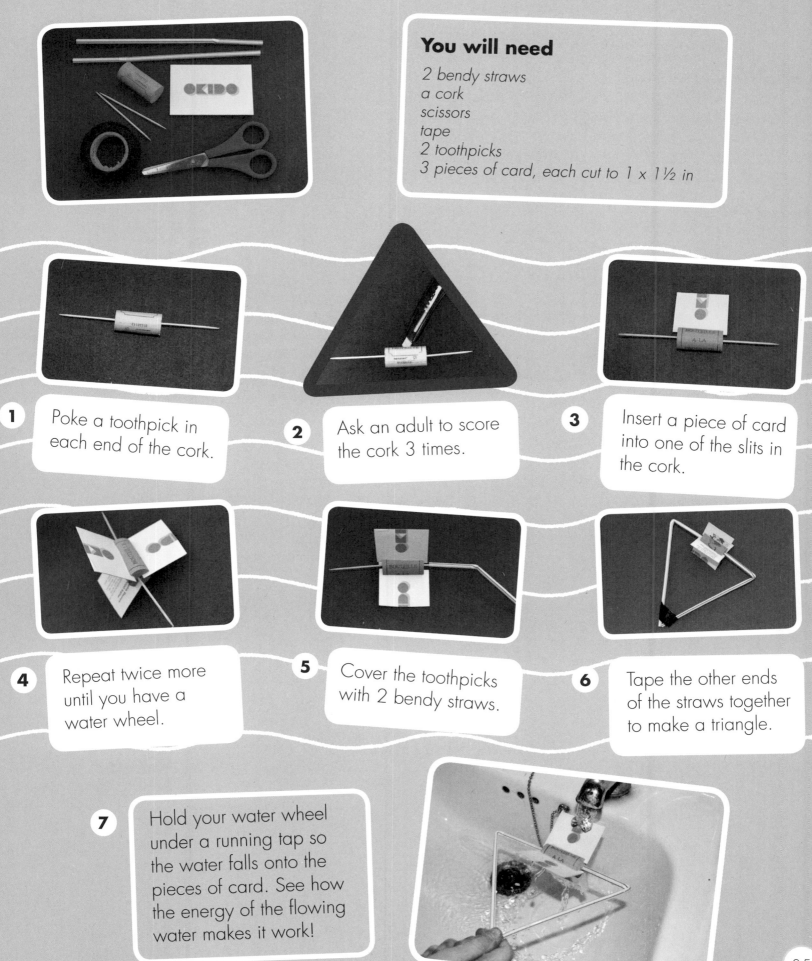

1 Poke a toothpick in each end of the cork.

2 Ask an adult to score the cork 3 times.

3 Insert a piece of card into one of the slits in the cork.

4 Repeat twice more until you have a water wheel.

5 Cover the toothpicks with 2 bendy straws.

6 Tape the other ends of the straws together to make a triangle.

7 Hold your water wheel under a running tap so the water falls onto the pieces of card. See how the energy of the flowing water makes it work!

35

Robot island

1 Far, far away, there was a tiny island …

2 … where two tribes of robots lived.

The Bababots   and   the Bobobots

3 The Bababots lived in Bababot village.

a Bababot

4 The Bobobots lived in Bobobot village.

a Bobobot

5 The Bobobots took their energy from a well of black oil deep in the ground.

6 The Bababots took their energy from the sun, wind and sea. These things can never run out.

7 One day, in Bobobot village …

Oh clang! It's not looking good!

Hurry up, I'm running low on energy!

8 The oil ran out!

9 The Bobobots slowed down then stopped!

Soo thirsty!

Need a fill-up!

10 Just one little Bobobot was still working …

Quick, Little Bobo, go to Bababot village!

They are the only ones who can save us! HURRY!!!

11 Little Bobo zoomed down to Bababot village …

12 The Bababots agreed to help!

Let's go!

13 The Bababots fixed the Bobobots with their tools. They made them solar panels, wind turbines and sea-wave machines!

14 The Bobobots threw a big party to thank the Bababots for saving them. From that day on, the Bobobots didn't need to worry about energy ever again!

Electricity

How does electricity get to your home?

Use your finger to follow the journey of electricity in the picture below.

Electricity is made in a **power station**. It travels to a **substation**, where it is made into high-voltage electricity. This means it can give out lots of power. Next it travels across **pylons** on overhead **power lines** to your home.

Electricity is dangerous. Never play with plugs and electrical gadgets!

start here

pylons   **substation**   **power station**

power lines

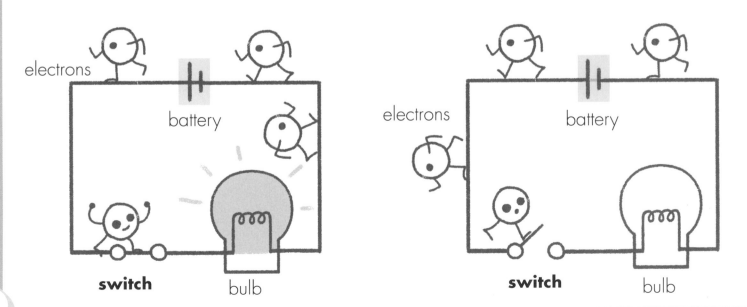

ON

To turn a light on, electricity needs to flow through wires in a loop, or circuit. When you flick the light switch down, you make the electricity flow.

electrons

battery

switch   bulb

OFF

To turn a light off, the flow of electricity through wires in the circuit needs to be broken. When you flick the light switch up, you break the flow.

electrons

battery

switch   bulb

Electricity makes all kinds of things around the house work. Follow the wires from the appliances to find out which ones aren't plugged in.

What is light?
Where does it come from?

Most light comes from the sun. It travels thousands of miles to reach Earth. This is natural light. When you switch on a flashlight, the electricity used to make the light comes from batteries made by people.

lightning
When lightning strikes, a flash of energy lights up the sky.

sun
The sun is the star that is closest to planet Earth.

fireflies
A firefly uses chemicals to make light with its body. It flashes its light to try and find a mate.

stars
A star is a huge ball of burning gas.

volcano
When a volcano erupts, burning-hot liquid explodes out and glows with light.

What kind of light?

Which of these things use natural light and which use light made by people?

light made by people

flashlight
A flashlight is powered with batteries.

fire
You can make a fire by burning wood. Fires can also start in nature without people making them.

car headlights
The headlights on a car are powered by electricity.

fireworks
Fireworks are made from gunpowder. Chemical reactions make them explode in colorful bursts of light across the sky.

Shadow play

What shape is your shadow? Have a look. It should be the same shape as you! When light cannot shine through a surface, it makes a shadow.

Let's trace shadows

You can make pictures called silhouettes by tracing around people's shadows. Try it out with a couple of friends!

You will need

flashlight

paper

pencil

putty

chair

2 friends

1 Stick a sheet of white paper to the wall with putty.

2 Sit on a chair near a wall. Turn so your body is sideways to the wall.

3 Ask one friend to shine a flashlight to make your shadow appear.

4 Ask another friend to trace the shape of your shadow. Swap over and do it again!

Drawing toy shadows

You can make all kinds of funny shadow shapes with a toy and a flashlight.

You will need

small toys

flashlight

paper

a friend

pencil

cardboard

1 Place a small toy on a piece of white paper on a table.

2 Ask your friend to hold the flashlight and shine it so a shadow appears.

3 Draw around the shadow.

4 Swap over and do it again!

What happens when you ...

... lie the toy down and shine the flashlight from above?

... stand the toy up and shine the flashlight from above?

... hold a sheet of white paper upright behind the toy?

... place the toy against an uneven surface?

43

What is sound?
Shout 'hello' really loudly!

You're making a sound. Do you like listening to music?
Music is sound, too. Sound can be quiet or noisy.

How is sound made?

Sound is made from vibrations,
or wobbles, in the air. The vibrations
travel in waves and reach our ears.

sound waves

A whistle makes a high sound.

A drum makes a low sound.

Adult help needed!

Play a glass orchestra

You will need

6 tall glass beakers
a big jug of water
a stick

What to do

1 Pour water into the glasses, as shown.
The first glass has no water, the
second has slightly more water, and
so on, until the sixth glass is full.

2 Gently tap each glass and listen.
What's the difference between the
sound each glass makes? Is it higher
or lower when there is less or more
water in the glass?

3 Have fun making lots of different
sounds. Invent your own tunes!

Make a string phone

You will need

2 paper cups
or yogurt containers

string

scissors

Adult help needed!

What to do

1 Ask a grown-up to cut a hole in the bottom of each cup or container.

2 Poke the end of the string through one cup or container, then tie a knot on the inside. Thread the other end of the string through the inside of the other cup.

3 Ask a friend to hold one cup to their ear while you speak into the other cup. What happens? Take turns speaking and listening.

Make a straw whistle

You will need

a glass of water
a drinking straw
scissors

What to do

1 Cut a little way through the straw without cutting it in two.

2 Hold the straw as shown in a glass of water. Blow gently.

3 Now gently raise and lower the straw in the glass. What happens to the sound?

Make a straw reed

You will need

a drinking straw
scissors

What to do

1 Flatten a drinking straw.

2 Snip off the end to make the pointed shape shown in the picture below.

3 Blow through this end until you make a sharp sound.

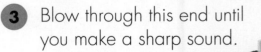

45

Musical families

Musical instruments belong to different families.
Each family of instruments makes sound in
a particular way.

**strings played with
a bow**

Strings   When you pluck an instrument with
your fingers, the strings vibrate. Ping!

plucked strings

mandolin   guitar   banjo   harp   violin   viola   cello   double bass

Spot all the musical instruments in the forest!
Are they in the wind, string or percussion families?

Wind

When you blow into a wind instrument, air vibrates inside a long tube. Oooom!

brass

bagpipes

recorder

trumpet   horn   trombone   tuba

woodwind

alpine horn

clarinet   flute   oboe   saxophone   pan flute

Percussion

You hit or shake a percussion instrument to make it vibrate. Bang!

drums   xylophone   triangle   bells

timpani   maracas   tambourine   cymbals

Keyboard Instruments

When you hit an organ key, air vibrates inside. Lah!

organ   piano

harmonica

accordion

concertina

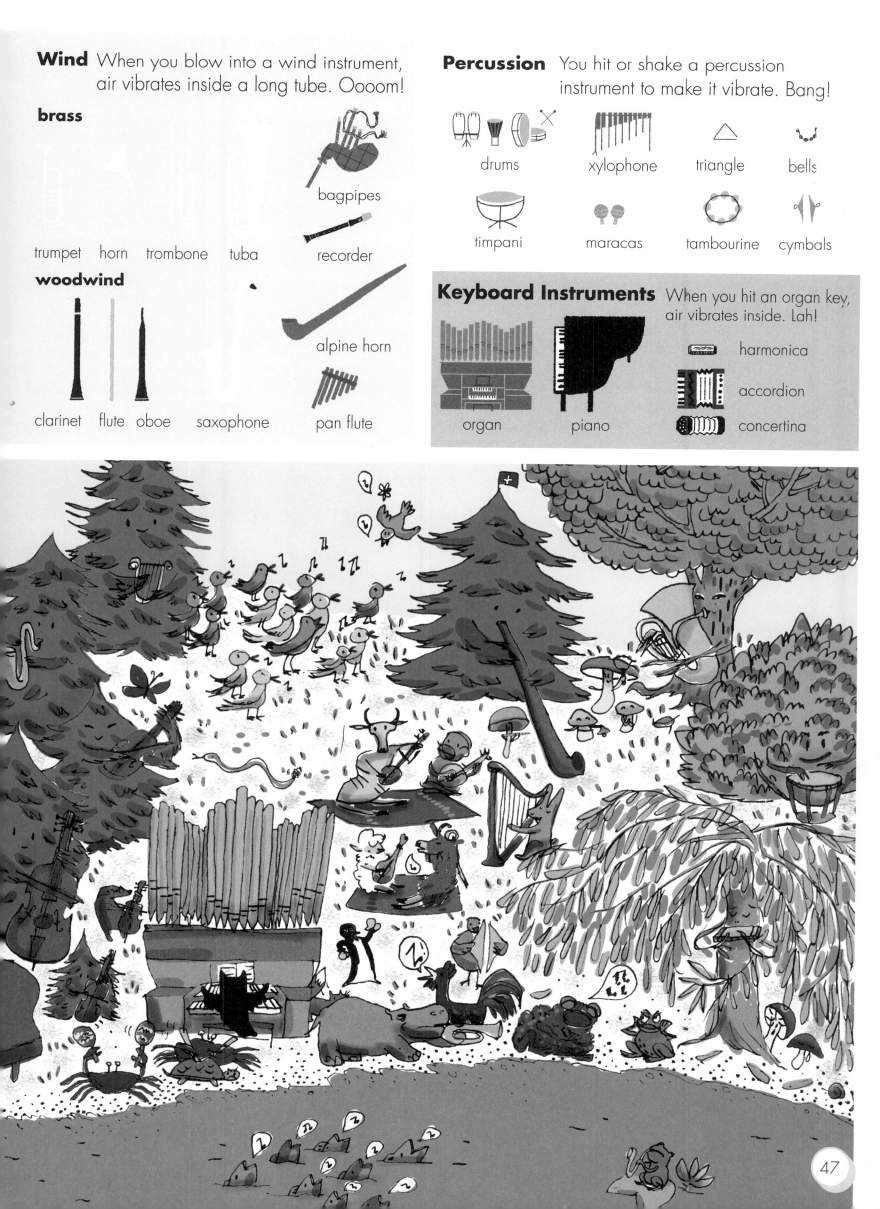

Let's measure
How big or small?

Look at the pictures. Which is the tallest: the robot, the person, the bus, the giraffe, the house, the tree or the high-rise building?

The high-rise building is just over 30 yards tall.

How many trees fit into the height of the high-rise building?

How many houses?

Giraffes?

Buses?

People?

Robots?

Footballs?

How tall are you? Measure yourself with a measuring tape.

Now close this book and measure roughly how many books tall you are! Ask an adult to help. Start at your toes and turn or 'fold' the book up your body until you reach the top of your head. How many books fit into your height?

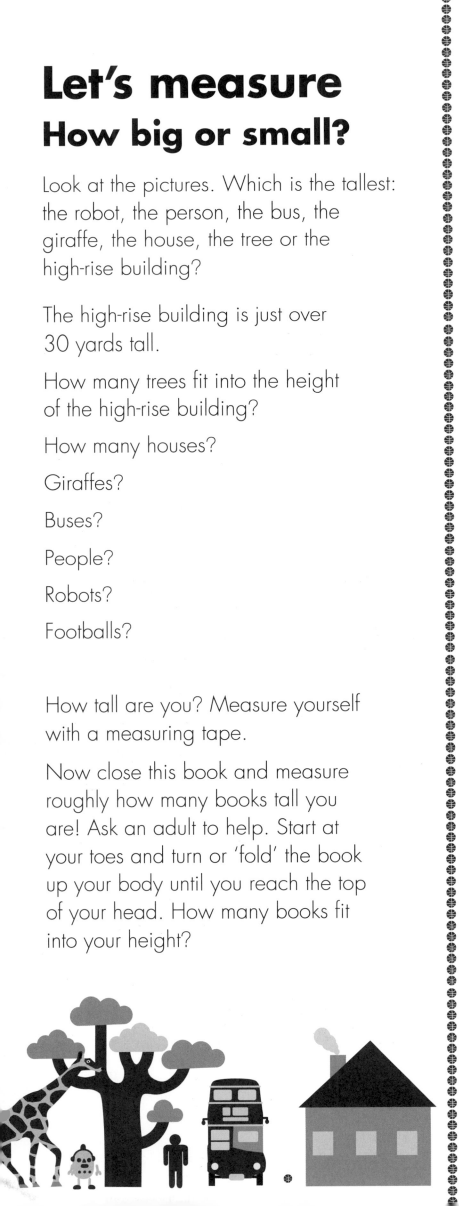

30 yd

height

25 yd

20 yd

15 yd

10 yd

5 yd

How heavy?

Scales are one way to find out how much something weighs. When scales balance, it shows that the objects on each side weigh the same amount.

Balancing the scales

Koko and Alex weigh the same.

A car is heavier than 3 explorers.

2 explorers are heavier than 1 explorer.

An explorer is lighter than a moped.

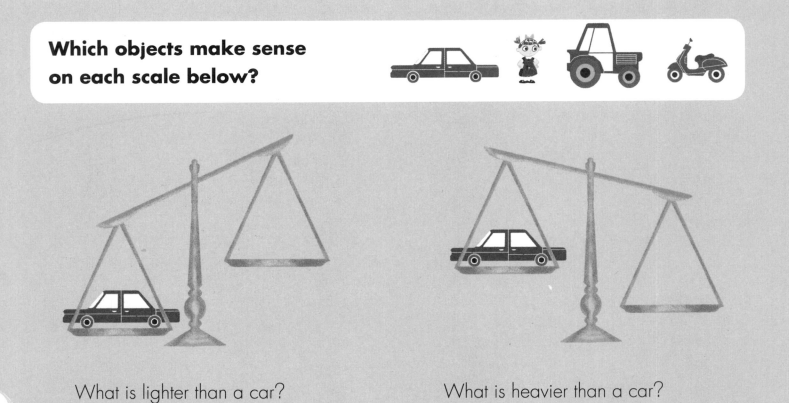

Which objects make sense on each scale below?

What is lighter than a car?

What is heavier than a car?

Make a mobile

Adult help needed!

You will need

string

scissors

masking tape

2 wire coathangers

colored card

hole punch

buttons and beads

1 Ask an adult to place one hanger through the other. Tape them together, as shown.

2 Continue to wrap the tape around the hangers until they are completely covered.

3 Cut out different-sized shapes from the colored card.

4 Ask an adult to make a hole in each of the shapes.

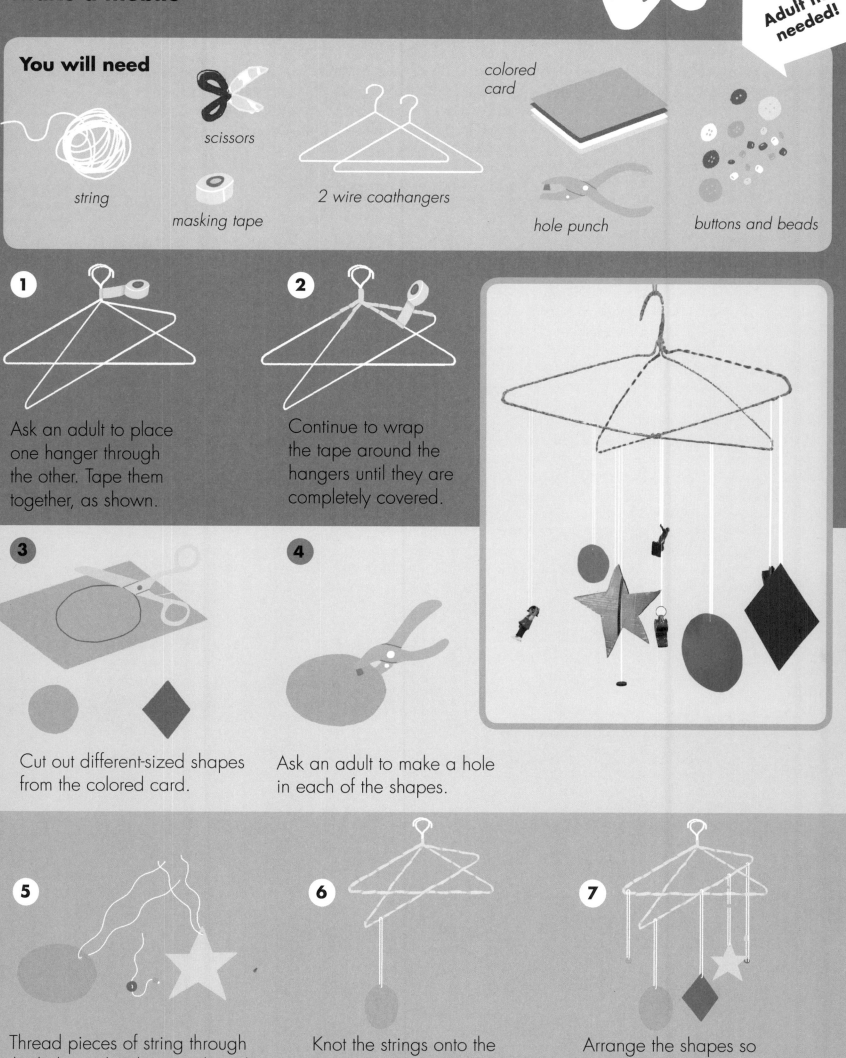

5 Thread pieces of string through the holes in the shapes. Thread beads and buttons, too!

6 Knot the strings onto the coathangers. Notice which shapes are heavier.

7 Arrange the shapes so the mobile balances.

On the move

Look at all the different kinds of transportation in this busy city. Everyone is on the move.

Beep! A **car** can take a family and all their bags to places nearby and far away. But it uses gas and can get stuck in traffic.

A **tram** runs on tracks on the road.

Toot! Toot! A **barge** chugs slowly up and down the river, delivering its load.

A **bicycle** is a quick way to reach places nearby. It doesn't use any fuel.

I love **walking**. There are no traffic jams and I use my own energy.

Who's going where?

Find these people in the picture. Help them choose the right type of transportation for their journeys. Are there other types of transportation they could also take?

Molly
I'm going to play in the park nearby.

Dad
I'm off to visit Grandma in Jamaica.

Smith family
We're going on vacation to the beach. We've got lots of bags.

Jones family
We're going to visit Auntie for the day. She lives near the train station in the next town.

Josh and Emma
Every morning, we need to get quickly to work on the other side of town.

A **van** has lots of space inside. It can travel nearby and faraway. But it uses gas and can get stuck in traffic.

An **airplane** flies thousands of miles across the world. It gets you to new places quickly but it uses lots of fuel.

A **train** runs on tracks across town and country. It carries many passengers at the same time.

A **taxi** is a quick way to get you exactly where you want to go. But it uses gas and can get stuck in traffic.

All aboard! A **bus** carries many passengers across town, from bus stop to bus stop.

A big **boat** sails to lots of places all around the world. It takes a long time.

Mind the doors! The **subway** runs underground. It takes many people across the city and avoids traffic jams.

Lily and her mom
We're off to town to go shopping.

Mrs. Potter
I need to deliver these boxes of tiles to the next town up the river.

53

How does a car work?

To make a car go, first you need to fill it up with gas. Then you have to turn the key in the ignition and press your foot on the accelerator. Beep beep!

The different parts of a car

Each part of a car has a special job.

The HAND BREAK stops the car from moving when it's stopped.

This is the EXHAUST pipe, where waste gases escape into the air.

The ACCELERATOR makes the car go faster.

Make a model car

Adult help needed!

Build cars with wheels made of corks or bottle tops. Race them on the floor with your friends.

You will need

4 straws	4 bottle caps or corks
tape	4 wooden skewers
putty	empty cartons or boxes

1

Push a skewer into each straw. Be careful of the sharp end!

2

Ask an adult to use c push pin to make a hole in the center of each bottle cap.

54

The driver uses the STEERING WHEEL to turn the car.

The BATTERY starts the engine and powers the lights.

The ENGINE powers the car and makes it go FAST!

A RADIATOR cools down the engine so it doesn't get too hot.

HEADLIGHTS help the driver to see when it is dark.

The BRAKE slows the car down.

3

Ask an adult to push the skewer-straw, sharp end first, through the holes in 2 bottle caps. Repeat so you have 2 sets of wheels.

You can also use corks for wheels.

4

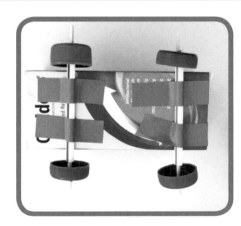

Lay the sets of wheels over the carton so they hang over the sides.

Tape the sets of wheels to the carton.

Turn it over and you have a moving car!

Decorate your cars and get racing!

People power
Who does what?

People have all sorts of different jobs. What job do you want to have when you grow up?

How to play
A game for 2 or more players

You will need
a die and game pieces

1 Place your pieces on START.

2 Take turns to throw the die and move along the board.

3 When you land on a person, jump to the job he or she is doing (hint: the colors match).

4 When you land on a job, jump to the person doing that job.

5 The first player to reach FINISH is the winner!

START

farmer

astronaut   **fisherman**   **teacher**

pilot

soccer player

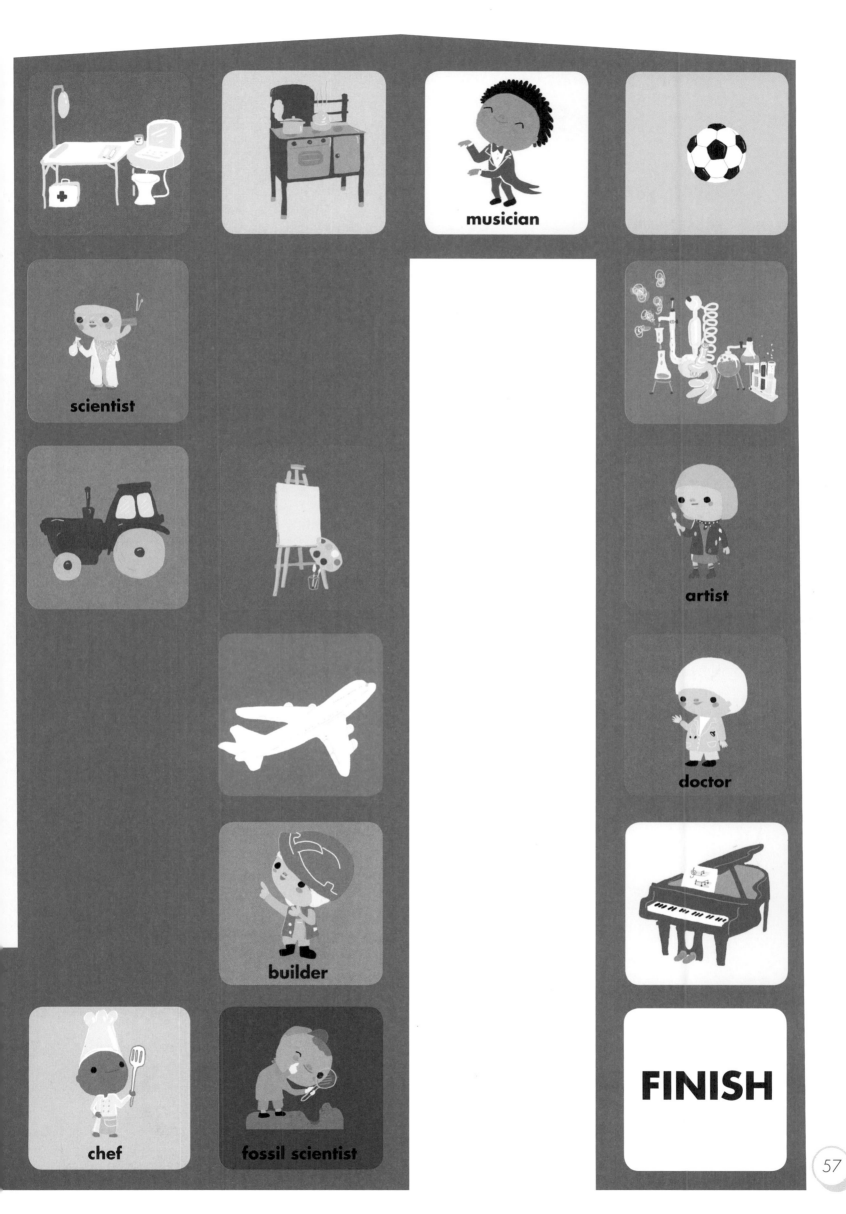

musician

scientist

artist

doctor

builder

chef

fossil scientist

FINISH

57

What's on TV?

Imagine presenting a TV show on Channel OKIDO. Would you like to be a scientist explaining how things work? Or a newscaster reading stories about the world?

Presenters perform in front of the cameras.

Writers work behind the scenes. They write scripts, which are the words that the presenters say.

Camera operators record videos that capture all the action.

Sound technicians record the sound. The presenters wear microphones to help with this.

The **lighting team** makes sure the light looks good and there are no shadows.

presenters

camera operator

Pictures from the studio are sent through cables to a **transmitter** …

… and then on to your TV via a **TV cable**, an **antenna** or a **satellite dish**.

TV cable

transmitter

antenna

lights

sound technician

satellite dish

Star on TV!

Adult help needed!

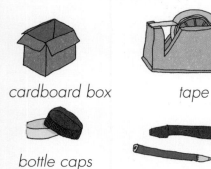

You will need

cardboard box

tape

glue

scissors

bottle caps

pens and pencils

mixed paper

Ask an adult to cut a large hole in one side of the box.

Use the materials above to make TV control buttons, microphones, a remote control, scenery and props.

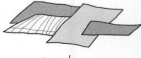

What shows will you make?

a nature show

a commercial

the weather forecast

the news

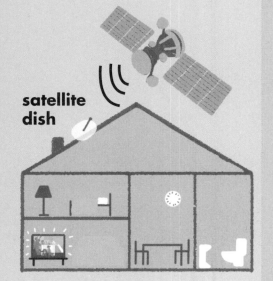

Play TV shows with a friend. What happens when he or she wants to change the channel?

Guten Tag!
Germany

Hello
United Kingdom

Buy a dictionary.

Move ahead to Germany.

Ciao
Italy

START

Privet
Russia

Hallo
Netherlands

Hello, hello!
Say 'hello' in 10 languages.

A game for 2 or more players

You will need a die and game pieces

How to play

1. Place your pieces on START.
2. Take turns to throw the die and move along the board.
3. When you pass a yellow space, say hello in the language.
4. When you land on a yellow space, say hello in the language and then jump to the next yellow space ahead.
5. The first player to reach FINISH is the winner!

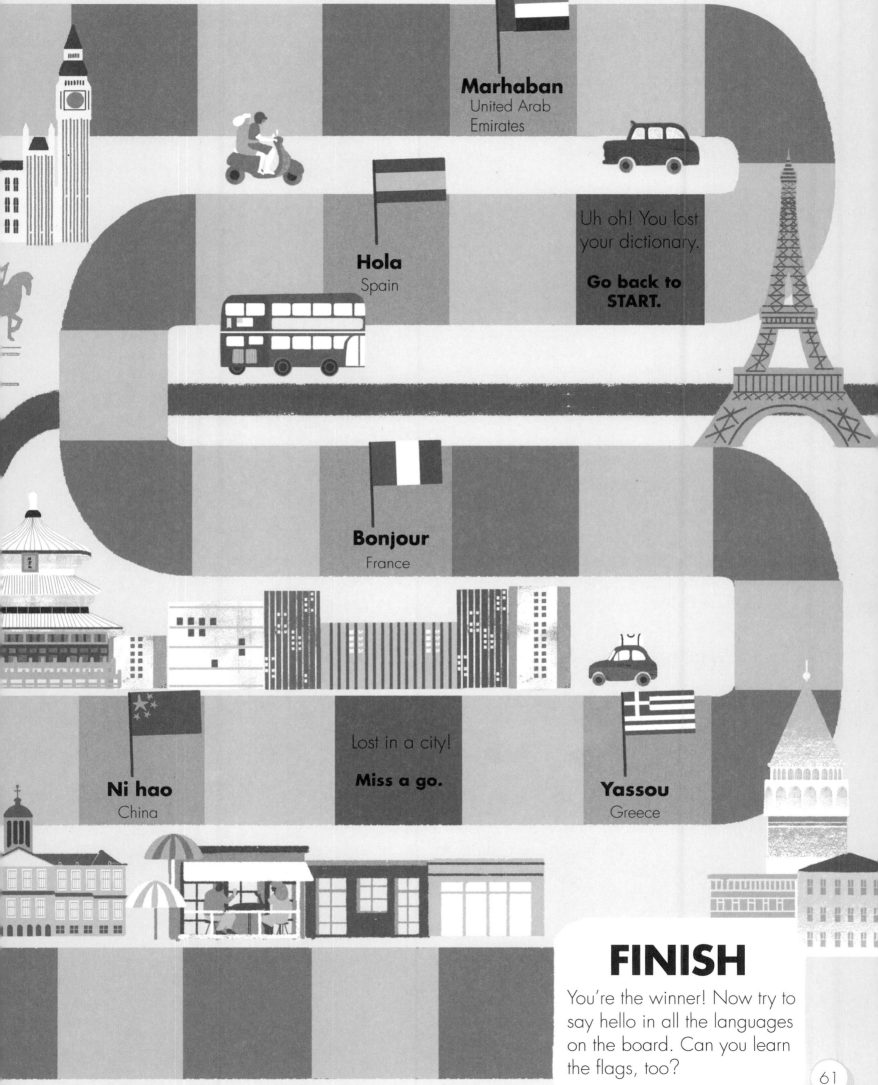

Marhaban
United Arab Emirates

Hola
Spain

Uh oh! You lost your dictionary.

Go back to START.

Bonjour
France

Ni hao
China

Lost in a city!

Miss a go.

Yassou
Greece

FINISH

You're the winner! Now try to say hello in all the languages on the board. Can you learn the flags, too?

Answers

Who lives where?
pages 10–11

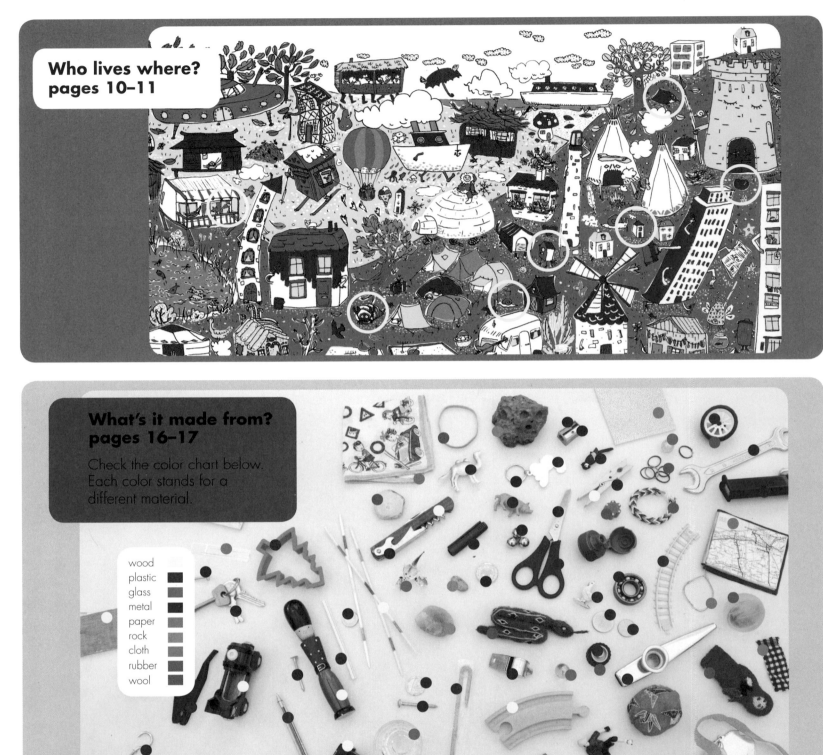

What's it made from?
pages 16–17

Check the color chart below.
Each color stands for a
different material.

wood
plastic
glass
metal
paper
rock
cloth
rubber
wool

Can you ride a bicycle made of wool?
pages 18–19

A hammer is
made of metal.

A suitcase is
made of plastic.

A bouncy ball is
made of rubber.

A sweater is
made of wool.

Glasses are
made of glass.

A bicycle is
made of metal.